#Team Bride

How to plan the
perfect party for your BFF

HarperCollins*Publishers*

HarperCollins*Publishers*
1 London Bridge Street
London SE1 9GF

www.harpercollins.co.uk

First published by HarperCollins*Publishers* 2019

13 5 7 9 10 8 6 4 2

© HarperCollins*Publishers* 2019

Illustrations © Shutterstock

Design and layout Sim Greenaway

Charlotte Brabbin asserts the moral right to be identified
as the author of this work

A catalogue record of this book is available from the British Library

HB ISBN 978-0-00-832055-3

EB ISBN 978-0-00-832056-0

Printed and bound in Great Britain by CPI Group (UK) Ltd, Croydon.

MIX
Paper from
responsible sources

FSC
www.fsc.org   FSC® C007454

FSC™ is a non-profit international organisation established to promote the
responsible management of the world's forests. Products carrying the FSC
label are independently certified to assure consumers that they come from
forests that are managed to meet the social, economic and ecological needs
of present and future generations, and other controlled sources.

Find out more about HarperCollins and the environment at
www.harpercollins.co.uk/green

#Team
Bride

Contents

Contents

Introduction

Let's Get This
Party Started!

What came first, the hen or the egg?
Actually, that's neither here nor there.
What we do know is that someone birthed
the hen party many moons ago, and
they've been very popular ever since.

The first official hen party took place
in Doncaster in 1872* when a woman
called Tracy Henthorn gathered together
some local housewives ahead of her
best friend's wedding. In full knowledge
that the hen is an ancient symbol for
nesting and fertility, Tracy took the ladies
to a nearby farm for a hen-plucking

(* Facts not verified.)

competition and encouraged them to fashion stylish headdresses out of the glossy feathers. It's encouraging to see Tracy's legacy continue today in the form of flower-garland and knicker-decorating workshops.

Since Tracy's day, the humble hen party's popularity has continued to flourish. You might remember your gran talking about raucous get-togethers at the bingo hall, and who can forget Auntie Shirley getting barred from the

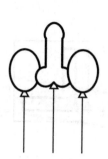

local Wetherspoons after repeated hen debauchery? The hen party has also flown the coop in recent years, branching out to destinations far and wide as ambitious millennials look to out-celebrate each other on social media. From Butlin's to Barcelona, there's a flag with a willy on it in pretty much every territory worldwide, and nobody is safe from the plucky broods of revellers in their bride squad armour. The hen party is already legend – and we wouldn't have it any other way!

#TEAMBRIDE

Of course, we all know there's no template for the perfect hen party. Every celebration will be unique – just like the lucky bride-to-be. Whether you're off for a relaxing spa weekend, indulging in a Tudor cooking class, tackling an inflatable obstacle course or planning a Big Night Out, your hen party will be loud and proud and individual. But whatever the order of the day, it's worth remembering that some things are sacred: it's the perfect time to bond with the bride's loved ones

ahead of the wedding, show the bride just how much she means to you and send her off in style as she embarks on her magical marital journey.

Whether you're a seasoned hen party attendee or still wearing your L plates, this is your go-to guide for planning the perfect celebration and learning how to be a top #TeamPlayer along the way! GO TEAM.

The
Hen Dos
and the
Hen Don'ts

Thou shalt not cock up the hen. Follow this simple etiquette guide and you won't need to worry about ruffling any feathers.

DO
Plan ahead. Failing to plan, as they say, is planning to fail!

DO
Consult your bride on the basics. Surprises are great, but not everything can be left to chance.

DO
Arrive well rested.
You want to bring your A game.

DO
Read the room. Not everyone
loves a stripper!

DO
Listen to your fellow hens.
Too many cooks and all that, but make
sure everyone feels included.

DON'T
Talk about the bride's partner's genitalia
too loudly in front of her mother-in-law.

DON'T
Steal the show. Remember, the bride is queen for the day!

DON'T
Get too competitive with the private anecdotes. We get it, okay. You all love the bride the most.

DON'T
Fall asleep in plain sight (unless it's designated nap time).

DON'T
Get arrested – this one is quite self-explanatory.

How to be a
#Team Player

Top Tips for the Bridesmaids

Congratulations, bridesmaids, you've got your call-up. It goes without saying that the smug phase *will* pass – the million WhatsApp notifications about big-day logistics will probably put paid to any complacency – but don't stress, you've got this do in the bag! And remember, there's a whole brood of fabulous, supportive hens right behind you.

◇ BUST A MOVE, NOT THE BANK
   You've got ideas galore, but remember that, unfortunately, you *can* put a price on fun. Know your budget from the beginning and work within your

means – best to avoid fights with angry hens when you have to ask them to cough up last-minute cash for that impromptu sky dive.

◊ GET H'APPY
There's an overwhelming amount of themed fun around when it comes to hen parties, but Pinterest is a brilliant source of inspiration and provides an easy method for collating all those ideas from the get-go. 'Appy days!

◊ NO HEN LEFT BEHIND
Chances are, not every guest will be able to make the party, but filming short video messages of any otherwise-engaged hens is a nice way to make

them feel involved, and a bonus surprise for the bride. (You could also get cardboard cut-outs of any AWOL friends, if you're feeling really fancy.)

◊ DARE TO DECORATE
Whether you're glamping, riding in a karaoke party bus or having a stay-at-home affair, a little decoration never goes amiss. And DIY decoration can be cheap and cheerful, too! Ask your hens to contribute everything from old photos of the bride, balloons and confetti to a pair of pants for the knicker bunting (a new pair ideally, but we're not here to judge). Think Linda Barker in *Changing Rooms* – you'll be amazed at how resourceful you can be.

◊ GROOMS ON FILM

It goes without saying that the hen party is strictly a spouse-free zone, but make sure you're 'Mr and Mrs' ready (see page 65). If the groom's game for this party pleaser – which he should be – call on him beforehand and put his relationship knowledge to the test. Perhaps it'll be sweet, perhaps it'll be excruciating ... Either way, watching back the Q&A will be top entertainment for your bride and her hens. The camera never lies!

◊ PICTURE PERFECT

It's one of the rare occasions when all the bride's favourite people will be in the same place together, so why not create a photo wall as a montage to the fun times with her besties! Pre-party, ask your hens to send over their favourite photos of the bride. No photo is too old or too embarrassing.

◊ NEXT STOP, PARTYVILLE
Perhaps this without saying, but make sure you've got the transport sussed way ahead of time. Getting from A to B sounds simple, but there's always one who ends up in Northampton when everyone else is popping prosecco in Northumberland. Also make sure you factor the transport into the original cost plan to avoid any grumbles – all-in means all-in!

◊ #TEAM
Get hashtag brainstorming! With any luck your hens will be having far too good a time to be glued to their phones during the celebrations, but having an individualised hashtag is a great way for everyone to share and find photos after the event. Remember to make it distinct (and not too smutty, who knows what might pop up online, literally ...).

◊ 'GIRLS ON TOUR'
Why not invest in some team tees to make everyone feel part of the gang? Cheesy? Perhaps. But T-shirts are guaranteed to bring nervous strangers together, not least as you can laugh

at all the crap nicknames on display.
Alternatively, think about personalised
badges, flip-flops, party hats, even
temporary tats ... anything that will
make a hen easily identifiable should
they prove a drunken flight risk.

Top Tips for the Hens

◊ YOU GUYS HAVE GOT IT EASY
What is there to do besides turn up,
love bomb the bride, be fun *enough*
that you'll give her lots of hilarious
memories but not so fun that she ends
up holding back your hair at 9 p.m.
It's true that the hens get the party
without the pressure, but we all know
that organised fun is – notoriously –

the best kind of fun, and there are a few things you can do to make sure that
a) the bridesmaids don't combust, and
b) the celebrations go down as smoothly as a Slippery Nipple cocktail (more on that later).

◇ GET CONNECTED
Don't be shy, it's time to reach out, ladies! If there are any hens that you haven't met before, why not ask the bridesmaids for their numbers or find them on Facebook before the do. Any solo hens who aren't attached to a group will be especially grateful, and it'll also help to put the bride at ease as her different social groups merge – less chance of fisticuffs at dawn!

◊ DON'T DRAG YOUR (HIGH) HEELS
Party planning is no easy feat, and chances are the bridesmaids have a hell of a lot of people/timetables/creative endeavours to carefully manage in the run-up to the hen. We've all got busy lives, but make sure you respond to the bridesmaids as speedily as you can – especially when it comes to pinning down a date and transferring over any funds. Get a gold star – or a gratuitous glass of prosecco – before the hen party's even started!

◊ THANK YOU FOR THE MUSIC
You can always bank on top tunes to bring people together. Depending on your mode of travel, why not create a top playlist of bangerz for the hen party

journey. You can hit play again during the actual celebrations, too, and dance until the sun comes up. Think Bruno Mars' 'Marry You', 'Run the World (Girls)' by Beyoncé, Madonna's 'Like a Virgin' and any power ballad classics. You'll be bonding with old-family-friend Rachel and singing into hairbrushes together in no time.

◊ FEEDING THE FIVE THOUSAND
If you're hitting the town, those stomachs need to be well lined, so think about what food or snacks you can bring to the table. If it's a large-scale hen party, the bridesmaids will be under pressure to deliver the goods in large quantities – nobody wants to

endure the wrath of a hangry hen —
so crack out that signature dish. Just
make sure you ask about any allergies
beforehand. And, make it known if
there are any special ingredients in
those brownies ...

◊ DOING IT PROP-ERLY
No matter what anyone says, fancy
dress is always a good idea ... right?
From props for the photobooth to silly
hat games to, well, just being fabulous
in that feather boa, a hen party is
the best excuse for raiding the old
fancy-dress box. You'll find some
gems (and perhaps lose your dignity
in the process).

◇ 'TAXI FOR LESLEY!'

At the risk of being over-prepared, why not get a few important phone numbers down – local taxi companies, the bridesmaids' digits, the local chicken joint – in case of emergencies. And perhaps make a physical list, too – true we're not in the Stone Age, but pavements do smash phones, and you might be grateful for that slip of paper in your bra at 2 a.m. While you're at it, carry a bit of cash, too – especially if your bride is a back-to-nature kind of gal. You won't find many cashpoints near those digital-detox yurts in the Surrey Hills.

◇ OH, BABY

Ah, isn't she a darling? Why not raid the family photo album, hens, and bring along a baby picture that you can use in a fun (and very wholesome) bridal party game? On arrival, pin your photo up on the wall or see if the bridesmaids want to collate all the snaps in one place. The bride can be tasked with matching each hen with their baby photo – and needless to say that there will be penalties for every incorrect guess. What could be cuter? (Or more creepy?)

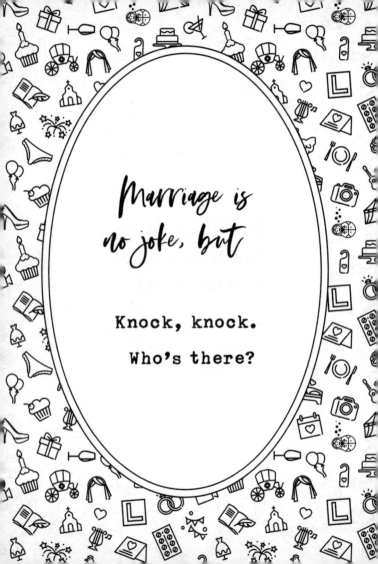

Marriage is no joke, but

Knock, knock.

Who's there?

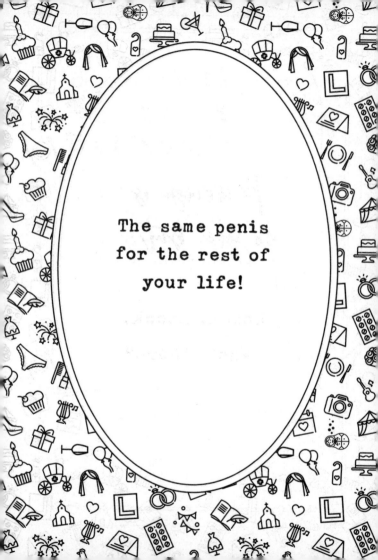

The same penis
for the rest of
your life!

Pre-Party Checklist

In a flap about packing? Fear not. Think of the following items as your hen party survival kit.*

- [ ] Your dancing shoes
- [ ] 1 packet of Pro Plus
- [ ] Scholl party feet
- [ ] Blister plasters aplenty

(* Not official government issue.)

- [ ] Willy water pistol
- [ ] 1 packet of Ibuprofen
- [ ] 1 tube of Berocca
- [ ] L plates
- [ ] Embarrassing stories of the bride to hand
- [ ] 1 spare pair of knickers (you never know)
- [ ] Willy whistle necklace
- [ ] Your dignity (remember you actually have to see these people again on the big day itself)

The Perfect Willy Cupcake Recipe

Very naughty and very nice, these delicious cupcakes really hit the sweet spot. Bake your way to pleasure town with this easy-to-follow recipe and take a batch of cakes to share at the hen party – the perfect quickie for elevenses or afternoon tea. This recipe involves a bit of careful icing for the decoration, but willy cake toppers and edible penis-shaped sprinkles are available online, if you'd prefer to keep things simple.

Ready, steady, bake!

Ingredients

Makes 12 cupcakes

FOR THE CUPCAKES

◊ 225g golden caster sugar
◊ 225g unsalted butter (at room temperature) or margarine
◊ 4 large eggs
◊ 1 tsp vanilla extract
◊ 225g self-raising flour
◊ 1 tsp baking powder

FOR THE VANILLA BUTTERCREAM

◊ 250g unsalted butter (at room temperature) or margarine

◊ ½ tsp vanilla extract
◊ 400g icing sugar
◊ A splash of milk
◊ Food colouring gels (optional)

FOR DECORATING

◊ Ready-to-roll royal icing (whichever colour tickles your fancy)

Equipment

◊ 12-hole cupcake tray and 12 paper cupcake cases
◊ Piping bag with plain/fluted nozzle (or even a small plastic bag with a small hole cut in the corner)

Method

1. Pre-heat the oven to 170°C/325°F/ Gas mark 3. Place 12 paper cases in your cupcake tray.

2. Take a large mixing bowl and beat the sugar and butter together until light and fluffy. You can use an electric whisk or simply mix by hand with a wooden spoon if you want to work on those triceps. Crack the eggs into a separate bowl and whisk. Slowly add to the sugar/butter mixture, making sure you beat as you go. Add the vanilla extract.

3. Next, sift in the flour and the baking powder and gently fold together

with a wooden spoon, or give a quick pulse with the electric whisk until just combined. Fill the paper cases evenly until they're about two-thirds full.

4. Bake in the oven for approximately 15 minutes, or until golden and a skewer inserted in the middle of the cake comes out clean. The sponge should feel light and springy (your naughty instincts may say otherwise but if they're rock hard, you've done it wrong). Allow the cupcakes to cool on a wire rack.

5. For the buttercream, beat the butter in a bowl for a few minutes until soft, and then add the vanilla extract.

Gradually sift in the icing sugar and fold into the butter mixture until light and fluffy. Add a splash of milk if it needs loosening. Drop in a touch of food colouring gel to the buttercream if you'd like to brighten things up.

6. Once the cupcakes have cooled, cut out a small piece of sponge from the centre of each using a small, sharp knife. Throw away (or eat) the excess cake and then fill in the 'holes' with a small dollop of vanilla buttercream. Don't over-stuff, we don't want it to be creaming everywhere ... Next, place a large scoop of the remaining buttercream in a piping bag and pipe in a neat swirl over each cupcake top.

7. Now comes the fun bit. Take your coloured royal icing and start to, well, craft a dozen little willies. There's no right or wrong here – the male genitalia, famously, comes in all shapes and sizes – but try to make them as uniform as you can. As a guide, roll out 12 little worms, 24 little pea-sized balls, then mould them together in a sort of phallic Frankenstein fashion.

8. Use a toothpick to create texture and grooves in the icing, if you're feeling ambitious. Place one willy on top of each cupcake – erect is probably best – and hey presto! Best served with tea, finger food and smutty stories about the bride.

Party Games

Surely no hen do is worth its salt without a bit of party-game action. You might have bigger activities planned depending on the scale of the celebrations, but if you're in need of an ice-breaker or eager to get your hen brood pumped ahead of a big night out, it's a good idea to have a few games up your sleeve. What's more, you can cater the festivities to match the bride's interests, showing her that you've thought of every detail.

So embrace the inner child (and the *devilish* woman) with this tailored list of party games, which are guaranteed hentertainment – whatever the vibe.

The Ones for the 'Sporty Bride'

◊ PENIS PIÑATA

You're probably up to your eyes in willies, but this one is a must-have. It's well hung and filled with sweet treats, so what's not to love? Each hen is blindfolded in turn, spun around and given a baton to swing at the piñata to release some goodies. Brilliant fun for the contestants, and the spectators. If you're feeling extra cheeky, why not fill the piñata with condoms, willy whistles and saucy sex toys instead of sweeties? Look out for the expression on the bride's face at the, er, explosion.

◊ SILLY WILLY HOOPLA

Remember playing that elephant Doh
Nutters game as a kid? Think of this
is as the X-rated adult version, where
you divide into teams and take it in
turns to 'hoop' coloured rings onto the
'target' – which looks suspiciously like
a penis. You can buy kits where you
lay the willy on a flat surface (what
an odd sentence), or those which
include a strap-on version (eh-up) for
your head. There are even 'light-up'
versions, so you can keep on tossing all
night long!

◊ BEACH OLYMPICS

You don't necessarily need a beach,
but you will at least need some sizeable
outdoor space for this one, and it's

probably better suited to a bride who really enjoys getting physical. Divide into teams and find out who's good in the sack with a good old-fashioned sack race, have a bounce on balloon boppers, get spooning with an egg-and-spoon race, and what better excuse to get up close and personal than a three-legged dash to the finish line? If the exertion gets a bit much, don't stress, as you can always resort to playing the wind-up racing willy game inside — all the competition, without the sweat!

The Ones for the
'Party Girl Bride'

◊ PROSECCO-PONG:

Keep it classy with balls and bubbles. This one is the glamorous cousin of the classic Beer-Pong game and it's a staple in the hen world for getting the party started. There are lots of kits available online that you can buy in advance, but all you need is twelve plastic glasses, three ping-pong balls, plenty of prosecco and lots of team spirit! Split the group into two teams and each hen gets a crack at landing their balls in the opposite triangle of cups. Every successful slam dunk means a drink, and the first team to get a ball in every glass wins. Let's get fizzy!

◊ POP IT LIKE IT'S HOT
If your hens haven't fully bonded yet, this game is guaranteed to bring them together – quite literally! All you need is a load of balloons, plenty of rhythmic energy and a playlist full of dance-floor classics to keep motivation high. Divide the hens into pairs and one hen in each couple should tie an inflated balloon around their waist. The aim of the game is to pop the balloon with a bit of close-and-personal dry humping. The first pair to pop three balloons between them wins. Your celebrations will go off with a bang!

◊ SHE SAID WHHHAAATT?

This game is brilliant fun whether you're out and about or partying at home. The bridesmaids set the rules here, choosing a few words that the hens are forbidden to say for a period of time – think 'wedding', 'party', 'ring', the groom's name, etc. If any hen makes a slip of the tongue, they have to do a forfeit as decided by the bridesmaid team. Whether they're downing their drink, taking off an item of clothing or challenging a stranger to a dance-off, actions will speak louder than words. Be warned that this one gets harder to judge if any slurring starts to occur ...

The Ones for the 'Creative Bride'

◊ PLAY-DOH PICTIONARY

Handsy and hilarious, this game is a race against the clock, but your hens won't want it to end. Divide into two teams and have one player from each pick a card from a pre-prepared deck. Every card will have a 'hen relevant' word – perhaps centred around weddings, willy synonyms, different sex positions – and the player must 'sculpt' the word out of a block of plasticine. The first team to guess the word correctly gets a point on the scoreboard. You'll have a lorra laughs, and maybe even discover the next Michelangelo!

◊ KNICKER BUNTING

Get crafty and pimp your pants with one of the cheekiest hen party activities going. You might want to book into an organised knicker customisation workshop, but the DIY version is brilliant fun, too. You can turn your hen party venue into a haberdashery palace with an endless supply of sexy sequins, bows, lace, buttons and pom-poms. Perhaps any willing hens could even bring a small photo of their other half to stick on the knickers (won't they be thrilled?). Just look out for the hen who thinks they can get away with making crotchless panties — it's lazy, and not the creative spirit we're after.

◊ PICTURE-PERFECT CUPCAKES

Again, the bridesmaids might be organising a more professional offering, but cupcake or cookie decorating is a deliciously good hen party ice-breaker, especially if the bride fancies herself as the next Mary Berry. Set up kitchen at hen HQ with tubs of buttercream, edible sugar paper, piping bags, sprinkles and even ice-tray willy moulds for crafting the perfect phallic topper! The icing on the cake to a perfect celebration, surely.

The Ones for the 'Saucy Bride'

◊ CONDOM COURGETTE

A healthy-sexy hybrid, this game is easy-peasy and guaranteed to set hearts racing. All you need is a few packs of Durex and some freshly sourced courgettes. Each hen is tasked with fitting the condom on the veg using only their mouth, and the first player to rubber up is the winner! Get ready for high concentration levels, and more sexual innuendos than you can shake a courgette at. Of course, you can use cucumbers or anything else of a similar shape that you can 'bag up' in the supermarket.

◊ GUESS THE BUM

It would be, well, a real bummer if you didn't have a crack at this party-game classic. Put the bride to the test and see if she can correctly recognise her fiancé's tush in a line-up of superior posteriors. The bridesmaids can either print off a batch of celebrity bums or ask each member of the stag party to supply a snap beforehand – naked or trousered up, it depends how brave you're feeling. Needless to say that the bride gets a forfeit if she picks the wrong behind. As games go it's not flash, but it's a right larf.

◊ COCK OR NOT

At a hen party, you call a willy a willy. But what if everything isn't as it seems? Don't worry, this isn't as biologically sinister as it sounds. The aim of the game here is to get a selection of pictures that could either be a pecker or, well, something more innocent. Think, I suppose, dodgy sweet potatoes, totem poles, sea anemones … Split your hens into teams and have them conduct an examination of the photos. This game is very hard (wheyyy), funny and guaranteed to sort the willies from the non-willies.

The Ones for the 'Basic Bride'

◊ TWERKIN' 9 TILL 5

Alright, basic bitches, forget the frills and discover that there's fun to be had in the most basic and budget of games. For this one all you'll need is a dozen ping-pong balls (woah, not where we're going, stop that filth), two empty tissue boxes and elastic straps for tying them around your hens' waists. Fill the tissue boxes with the balls, put on 'Anaconda' by Nicki Minaj, and twerk it like there's no tomorrow. The first hen to empty their box of balls is the winner!

◊ LIKE A MUPPET ON A STRING

Arguably the queen of all basic bitch games. Your toolkit? A piece of string, a banana and a satsuma (no prizes for guessing where this is going). Divide the hens into teams and tie a piece of string around each player's waist and add the banana so that it's hanging down between their legs. Place a satsuma in front of each player and, using only their hips, the hens have to gyrate and swing the banana to hit the satsuma. Think smutty mini golf. The goal is to get the satsuma to a 'finish line' and then back again in relay-style. The winning team is the first with every hen back at the start. This one is thrust-heavy and tiring, but you can hand out the fruit at the end as a nutritious snack!

◊ HOLD ON TIGHT
Make sure you capture this on film because it's going to have your hens in stitches. All you need to do is buy a bunch of tights (no need for any sexy stocking nonsense) and put them in the middle of the room. Distribute some oven mitts among your hens and, when the head bridesmaid gives the signal with a blow on their willy whistle, the hens must grab a pair of tights and try their best to pull them on with their oven-mitted mitts. Not quite as easy as it sounds and, basically, hilarious.

SCORES/NOTES

_____
_____
_____
_____
_____
_____
_____
_____
_____
_____
_____
_____
_____
_____
_____
_____
_____
_____
_____
_____
_____
_____

SCORES/NOTES

_____

_____

_____

_____

_____

_____

_____

_____

_____

_____

_____

_____

_____

_____

_____

_____

_____

_____

_____

SCORES/NOTES

_____
_____
_____
_____
_____
_____
_____
_____
_____
_____
_____
_____
_____
_____
_____
_____
_____
_____
_____
_____
_____
_____

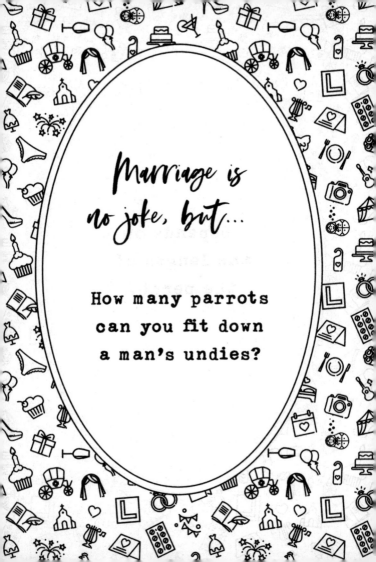

Marriage is no joke, but...

How many parrots
can you fit down
a man's undies?

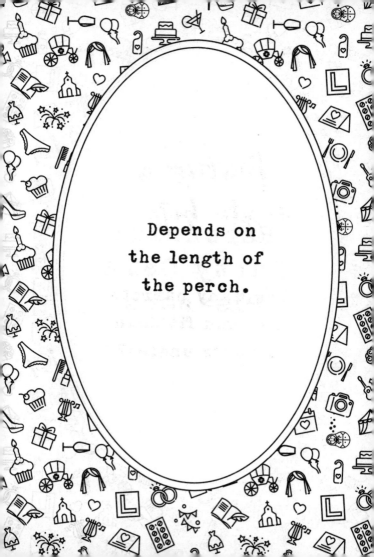

Depends on
the length of
the perch.

Perennial
Party Game
Pleasers

Think of these party games as the most-played in the hen party Greatest Hits album. They may not be the most surprising or unique, but they certainly please the crowd. So go on, top off your hen do with these evergreen classics.

Mr and Mrs

Finally, your opportunity to channel Philip Schofield! Who will come out on top in the battle of the sexes? (And, of course, Mr and Mrs is the name of the game as we know it, but the same formula applies if you're creating a Mrs and Mrs version!)

There's a good chance that the bridesmaids will be well prepared for this ever-popular quiz game – the tech-savvy among them might have even captured the bride's partner's answers on film in advance, ready for their hen party television premiere. But if a more spontaneous game is the order of the day, get the groom on speed dial pronto and sit the bride down with a glass of something strong. Remember, once the bride has given her final answer to each of your questions, reveal the groom's response to see if she's correct.

If she isn't, well, why not give her a shot as a forfeit, or make her play Truth or Dare. Non-mandatory, but excitement levels will rise along with the stakes!

It's a nice idea – and infinitely funnier – to make your quiz as personal to the happy couple as you can, but here are a few questions to get you started:

◇ What was your partner's first ever job?
◇ Who's the better kisser?
◇ Who is the messiest?
◇ What three words would you use to describe your partner?
◇ What would your partner grab first in a fire?
◇ What's your partner's worst habit?
◇ Who is their celebrity crush?
◇ Where did you go for your first date?
◇ Who takes the longest to get ready?
◇ Who snores the loudest?
◇ Where's the most adventurous/strangest place you've had sex?
◇ What are your pet names for each other?
◇ What is your partner's favourite sex position?

◊ What is your partner's ultimate saucy
   fantasy? (Feel free to give multiple
   choices here: think milk maid, cheerleader
   or naughty nurse.)

IF YOU WANT TO GET REALLY DEEP ...

◊ Who said 'I love you' first?
◊ Who is most nervous about the big day?
◊ How many children does your partner
   want?
◊ Who will be the first to cry on your
   wedding day?

Toilet Paper Couture

If there's a lull in the fun or if you need to flush away any awkwardness in the hen party atmosphere, look no further than everyone's favourite team game. All you need is a few rolls of toilet paper, cellotape, the competitive sass of RuPaul and all of your imaginative powers to create the perfect 'wedding dress'.

Divide your hens into teams by picking names out of a hat, and have each team nominate a 'bride'. The real bride can act as competition judge if she fancies, or perhaps she'd like to be one of the models – if anything, this'll only help to reinforce the quality of her real wedding day finery and make her appreciate it all the more!

When it comes to crafting a bog-standard wedding dress, there really are no rules. You might go for a strapless classic or an off-the-shoulder number, or really test your skills with a big, puffy Princess Andrex look. Whatever your taste, let the hilarity and the healthy competition ensue, and give your hens 15 minutes on the clock to perfect their creations.

And if you're really confident in the durability of your dresses, why not hit the runway? A hen fashion show makes for a hilarious section of the photo album. All those hours spent binge-watching *America's Next Top Model* and *Project Runway* are about to pay off.

Hen Charades

Right, ladies, it's time for a little role-play. Charades is perhaps best known for tearing families apart at Christmas time ('I said it had three syllables, THREE!!'), but it's a versatile game, and will push even the most patient players to their limit, so perhaps a good one to call on if your hen party is looking that bit too happy and harmonious … Only joking! (Sort of.) This classic will have your hens bonding – and shouting animatedly – in no time, and it'll also likely have them in stitches owing to the odd saucy twist.

Divide the hens into teams – keep the numbers smallish at three or four to a team – and have them take it in turns to act out something 'hen-ish' or 'sexy' or 'wedding' related in their chosen category for the rest of their team. Ready-made hen-do charade sets are available to buy online – and some even have conveniently mini cards that you can squeeze into your clutch bag, ready to whip out during a big night out. But if you're after some spontaneity – and you feel like channelling your inner artiste – you can simply write out your themed words of choice on colourful card and hand them out to each team.

Here are a few starter ideas to get you hot under the collar. This acting malarkey can be quite tough going, so it's strongly advised that you have plenty of willy cupcakes (see page 34) close by to keep the hen squad energised and at peak performance!

FILMS

- ◊ *The Full Monty*
- ◊ *My Big Fat Greek Wedding*
- ◊ *Four Weddings and a Funeral*
- ◊ *Magic Mike XXL*
- ◊ *Dirty Dancing*
- ◊ *Octopussy*
- ◊ *The Runaway Bride*
- ◊ *Bridesmaids*
- ◊ *My Best Friend's Wedding*
- ◊ *Snakes on a Plane*
- ◊ *Great Expectations*

BOOKS

- ◊ *Lady Chatterley's Lover*
- ◊ *Fifty Shades of Grey*
- ◊ *Riders* – or anything by Queen Jilly Cooper
- ◊ *Tipping the Velvet*
- ◊ *Middlesex*
- ◊ *Dracula* (it gets pretty erotic, OK?)
- ◊ *Forever*
- ◊ *Twilight*
- ◊ *Lace*
- ◊ *Bridget Jones's Diary*

SONGS

- ◊ 'Bump N' Grind'
- ◊ 'Sexual Healing'
- ◊ 'No Diggity'
- ◊ 'Hungry Eyes'
- ◊ 'Sex on Fire'

- ◊ 'Low'
- ◊ 'Lady Marmalade'
- ◊ 'You Sexy Thing'
- ◊ 'Smack That'
- ◊ 'Love in This Club'
- ◊ 'Hot Stuff'

SEX POSITIONS (maybe use a pillow
for this one, rather than an unwilling hen!)

- ◊ Doggy style
- ◊ 69
- ◊ Cowgirl
- ◊ Missionary
- ◊ The Scissors
- ◊ Spooning
- ◊ Reverse Cowgirl
- ◊ The Eagle
- ◊ The Wheelbarrow

MISCELLANEOUS

◇ Stag do
◇ Maid of Honour
◇ Throwing the bouquet
◇ Best man's speech
◇ Mother-in-law
◇ Honeymoon
◇ Something borrowed
◇ First dance
◇ Wedding breakfast
◇ Cutting the cake

SCORES/NOTES

_____
_____
_____
_____
_____
_____
_____
_____
_____
_____
_____
_____
_____
_____
_____
_____
_____
_____
_____

Cocktail
Recipes

Whether you're getting warmed up for a big night out or having a hens' night in, make sure you toast the occasion with a cocktail or two. These recipes are bang on theme and will make Happy Hour a hit if you're running your own hen party cocktail bar.

Note: if there are any arguments over who's making the next batch, you can always draw penis straws – whoever gets the short one, really does lose.

And remember to drink responsibly hens!

Sex on the Beach

A classic, and a hen party must-have.
You'll get all the pleasure – and none of
the sand in places it shouldn't be ...

Makes 1 (multiply by 4 to make up a jug)

INGREDIENTS

◊ A selection of tall glasses
◊ Ice cubes
◊ 35ml vodka
◊ 9ml peach schnapps
◊ 35ml orange juice
◊ 35ml cranberry juice
◊ Orange slice and maraschino cherry,
  to garnish

METHOD

1. Fill a tall glass with ice cubes. Add all of the ingredients into a cocktail shaker and shake well.
2. Pour the fruity liquid into the glass. Garnish with the orange slice and cherry. Now put on that old hit by T-Spoon and dance away with glass in hand. C'mon, move your body!

Penis Colada

Who's got a lovely bunch of coconuts?
Tropical and fruity, you'll be transported to
the Caribbean in no time.

Makes 1 (multiply by 4 to make up a jug)

INGREDIENTS

◇ A selection of tall glasses
◇ Ice cubes
◇ 5 chunks of pineapple
◇ 1 tsp sugar
◇ 1 tbsp coconut cream
◇ 50ml golden rum
◇ 70ml fresh pineapple juice

◊ Juice of ½ lime
◊ Pineapple triangle, maraschino cherry and cocktail umbrella, to garnish

METHOD

1. Fill a tall glass with ice cubes. Place all your ingredients, except the lime juice, into a blender and blitz until a smooth consistency. Taste and add a splash of lime juice as required.
2. Pour into the chilled glass, add your garnish and serve. Grab a glass, put on some party hits and get ready to rum-ble!

Bell(end)ini

This one's just peachy. Why not have a fluteful at breakfast and start as you mean to go on? It'd be rude not to.

Makes 8

INGREDIENTS

◊ 200g tinned peaches in fruit juice
◊ 8 champagne flutes
◊ 1 bottle of prosecco or champagne
◊ 1 peach, thinly sliced, to garnish

METHOD

1. Add the tinned peaches and their juice
    to a blender and blitz for a minute or
    so until smooth. Put the peach purée
    into a champagne flute until the glass
    is about a third full, then gently top up
    the glass with prosecco or champagne.
2. Garnish the flute with a slice of peach
    and serve. If you don't want the hassle
    of blending, you can always buy
    ready-made peach purée. Why add
    any fuss to the fizz?

Slippery Nipple

More of a shooter than one to be sipped, this drink goes down a treat. Bottoms up, ladies!

Makes 1

INGREDIENTS

◊ 7.5ml grenadine syrup
◊ A healthy supply of shot glasses
◊ 20ml sambuca
◊ 20ml Baileys (or other Irish cream liqueur)

METHOD

1. Start with the 'nipple' of the cocktail by adding the small amount of grenadine to the bottom of a shot glass.
2. Float the sambuca on top and then add the Baileys as the final layer. Short, sweet and creamy, this treat will have you coming back for more. Just be careful of any spillages among all the excitement: you don't want any accidents due to a slippery nipple floor.

Dares for
Dummies

As they'd say in *Gladiators*, 'Hens, are you reeeaddddyy?' This one's especially good if you're planning a big night out on the town. Raise the party stakes and collect hen points for every dare successfully completed in this checklist. The hen who collects the most points by the end of the night will be crowned 'Top Hen'. And perhaps there's a prize waiting for them at the end of a sticky, penis-confetti-strewn bar table ... Offer up some chocolates, a pamper kit or even a small willy-shaped trophy for the victor.

Bring it on, Mother Clucker!

☐ Ask someone for their autograph
  1 point

☐ Get a selfie with a bouncer
  2 points

☐ Convince someone you're a spy
  (worst spy in history)
  3 points

☐ Chat someone up in a foreign accent and
  convince them you're from that country
  4 points

☐ Photobomb a stag do
  5 points

☐ Propose to a barman
   6 points

☐ Swap an item of clothing
   with a total stranger
   7 points

☐ Fake a very loud orgasm
   8 points

☐ Kiss a bald man on the
   top of his shiny head
   9 points

☐ Start a flash mob
   Top banana – 10 points

Top Tips
for Hen
Emergencies

'*Did someone call the police?*' With any luck, that'll be the cue for someone to crack on the *Full Monty* soundtrack and for a well-oiled, truncheon-bearing fella to dance into the room, crotch first – rather than it being the signal for an official police raid of the hen premises. But, that's not to say that you shouldn't be prepared in the event of a real-life hen emergency. You want the group to be joking about 69s, not dialling 999. You're after a criminally good time, not a criminal record.

So, think of this list of 'How-Tos' as your hen party insurance policy. You'll be ready to rescue the celebrations at the very first sign of drama.

CODE
THREAT LEVEL

MILD

MODERATE

SEVERE

How to Keep the 'Rowdy Hen' in Check

We all know the one. The good-time gal who's a real hoot, but occasionally takes things a step too far. Like a toddler who refuses to go to bed, it's all fun and games until she gets over-tired and ends up having a public paddy on the floor, while removing inappropriate items of clothing. But there are ways to counteract this. Choose a few designated spies in the party squad – perhaps a bridesmaid and a close friend of the rowdy hen – who can keep a careful watch on her excitement barometer. Early warning signs to look out for include:

1. Raised noise levels
2. Heel tottering
3. Bad-mouthing fellow hens
4. Sky rocketing confidence levels
5. Greenish skin tones

You can avert full-scale meltdown by steering the rowdy hen away from the main group for a while ... and perhaps getting her a pint of water. The bride will be none the wiser and can keep on partying until dawn!

How to Beat Off
Unwanted Attention

Let's face it, the energy in a hen party can be dangerously infectious. You're laughing, catching up on old times, basking in the bride's pre-marital glow ... And a troop of super-sexy hens out on the tiles? Irresistible! But do be wary of clingers. Those characters who don't just jump into the fray for one stop but want to join in for the Whole. Damn. Ride. And they can be handsy, too. But remember that there's strength in numbers, and a hen group is well equipped to shake off these limpets. Why not form a hen barrier if you're out in a bar or club, dancing closely in formation to shut off any entry points – your very own special form of cock-blocking. And although it can be very nice when people offer to buy you drinks, be wary about accepting that complementary bottle of prosecco from 'Steve and the lads' at the far table – give 'em an inch and they'll take a mile and all that.

How to Rouse
the 'Lazy Hen'

It's an unwritten rule that the modern hen party is a marathon, not a sprint. Increasingly, the celebrations can last for a whole weekend, and sometimes even longer, so hens can certainly be excused for needing a moment of 'down time'. A hen wants to break away from the group for a stroll or grab a power nap? No problem! We can't be keen beans all the time, but there's lazy, and then there's lazy. It isn't uncommon to have a disengaged hen who just doesn't pull their weight. Perhaps they never offer to make the next pot of tea, shirk 'official photographer' duty or make a break for bed without offering to clear up the evening's detritus. Re-engage them by thinking about their strengths and interests. Perhaps they're a whizz on the DJ decks – so put them in charge of the playlist. Perhaps they love admin (it happens) – so put them in charge of itinerary timings and taxi ordering. Unfortunately, a leopard never changes its spots. But you can put them in a onesie and order them to have a good time!

How to Manage Tricky Mothers-in-Law

The mother-in-law. Perhaps the most revered and feared member of the hen do squad. But don't panic. And whatever you do, don't look her directly in the eyes.

But jokes aside, it's all about being sensitive to the bride's needs and taking time to understand her relationships with the hen party members. Perhaps she'll want to break things up and have a separate celebration with mum and her mother-in-law to be. But if the bride is keen to have a one-size-fits-all hen party, step up the bridesmaids: the umpires in this tricky game of emotional ping-pong! If the mother-in-law displays early signs of overbearing, vocal behaviour, there are ways of managing the expectations around her role – and making sure that the bride stays as stress-free as possible! Give Mum and Mother-in-law a careful run-down of the itinerary well in advance. This will help to avoid the stress of the unexpected, and you'll also show them who's running this gig. On advice from the bride, why not also gently suggest alternative activities. If they're game for a big night at *Magic Mike Live* – terrific! But if it's not their cup of tea, you could literally steer them in the direction of one ... Point out afternoon tea spots in the area, or cafés where they could hang out during the more risqué hen activities. There's no golden rule when it comes to managing hen party politics, but you can do your research beforehand. Remember – knowledge is power ...

How to Defuse Any Hen Tension

In an ideal world, everyone would rub along perfectly and the hen party video reel would look like an outtake from a *High School Musical* crescendo number. But all-singing, all-dancing harmony sadly isn't a given – especially if perfect strangers and one too many alcoholic tipples collide. So if you sense a bit of tension in the air, why not turn to those quiz games and group activity ideas to lighten the atmosphere? (See pages 42–76.) A simple game of Toilet Paper Couture is guaranteed to bring people together, and who wouldn't have a laugh at a round of Guess the Bum? It's true you shouldn't put too much pressure on the group to have the BEST TIME EVER – remember that you can't force the hens to be best buddies. But you can help everyone feel included and encourage a bit of #TeamBonding. And if you're really struggling? Fake it till you make it and pull people together for some group snaps – 'Everyone smile!'

How to Help a Bride
with Cold Feet

It's the moment that every hen dreads. You see it happen in the movies, but surely, surely, no bride actually has the 'I-can't-do-this' freak-out moment in the middle of her hen party, tearing off her sash and hyperventilating into a paper bag while one of the bridesmaids discreetly escorts her into the Ladies? And chances are, a melodramatic meltdown really is very unlikely. But if the bride does display any symptoms of cold feet, then reassurance is key.

Escort her away from the main group and take the time to listen, and remind her it's all part of a natural pre-wedding pattern. Reiterate that pre-wedding jitters are completely normal – almost to be expected. After all, she's saying adieu to her single status forever. She's staring down the barrel of the same penis for the rest of her days. She's got all that bleedin' paperwork to sort out if she decides to change her name. And, of course, all the pressure of planning a wedding is enough to raise even the most stubborn of stress levels. So, slapping her round the face with an inflatable willy and telling her to 'Get a grip!' isn't going to help anyone.

Note, too, that a hen party perhaps isn't the best time to ask the bride any 'difficult questions' – no big decisions can be made where cocktails and butlers-in-the-buff are involved. Most importantly, just help your bride to relax and unwind. And if you have to distract her by taking off your top and challenging a rival stag party to a dance-off, then so be it.

*Marriage is
no joke, but...*

There was a young
man from Perth,
Who was of
unusual girth.

He was as thin
as spaghetti,
But when he was
forking with Betty,
His meatballs
made her cry out
in mirth.

Thanks for
the Memories!

+

4eva

Fun and laughter is often the order of the day at a hen do, but there's also a lorra love to celebrate.

The bride-to-be has chosen you to accompany her on her final leg as a single lady. You're her homie, her comrade in life and love, and boy is that an honour! So now comes the cheesy bit ...

It's time to reflect on your own love story with the bride, using these quizzes and keepsakes as an ode to your unique friendship – showing her just how much she means to you. Let's hope there are plenty of penis-adorned tissues in those hen party bags ...

A Whole Lot of History

The groom who? Forget that fella for a moment. This is about you and the bride. Hoes before bros, sisters before misters ... This is just a small footnote in the history of your epic friendship, but we'll keep things light for now. So, cast your mind back and answer these fun questions about your bloody brilliant bride-to-be.

Why not then have the bride read the answers aloud and guess 'who said what'? You can *of course* give the bride a forfeit for anything she answers incorrectly (you get the drill by now). Just remember that excessive shot taking is a sure-fire way to make her fall flat on her face down memory lane ...

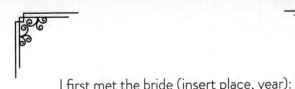

I first met the bride (insert place, year):

_____

_____

_____

_____

_____

The first thing I said to the bride was (don't worry if you can't remember, this is a toughy, especially for those primary school pals!):

_____

_____

_____

_____

_____

_____

I first knew she was a good egg when:

_____

_____

_____

_____

_____

_____

_____

The best day out/holiday the bride and
I have ever had was:

_____

_____

_____

_____

_____

_____

_____

The funniest memory I have of the bride is:

_____
_____
_____
_____
_____
_____
_____
_____

She made me feel better when:

_____
_____
_____
_____
_____
_____
_____
_____
_____

I'll never forget the time she:

_____

_____

_____

_____

_____

_____

_____

_____

The thing I love most about her is:

_____

_____

_____

_____

_____

_____

_____

_____

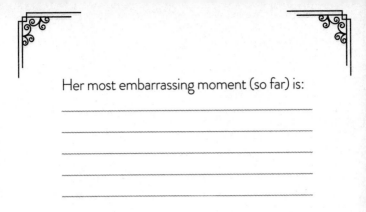

Her most embarrassing moment (so far) is:

_____
_____
_____
_____
_____
_____
_____
_____

If I had to use three words to describe her,
they'd be:

_____
_____
_____
_____
_____
_____
_____
_____

If the bride was an animal, she'd be:

_____

_____

_____

_____

If the bride and I had our own first dance,
our song would be:

_____

_____

_____

_____

She really surprised me that time she:

_____

_____

_____

_____

She was really annoying that time she
(don't sharpen the claws too much here):

_____
_____
_____
_____
_____
_____

If our love story was a Disney film, it
would be:

_____
_____
_____
_____
_____
_____
_____
_____

Trust Me, I'm a Hen! —
The Gift of Good Advice

'Don't eat yellow snow.' 'A bird in the hand is worth two in the bush.' 'Don't count your chickens/hens before your eggs have hatched ...'

All idioms worth saying, I'm sure, but now time for some slightly more wedding-specific advice. The bride has bought her 'wifey is for lifey' T-shirt, and she needs to know that her Agony Aunt hens have her back as she preps to walk down the plank – ahem, sorry – the aisle towards a lifelong commitment with her lucky chap.

It takes a village to raise a baby, but it takes a hen brood to support a marriage (said nobody, until now). So here's your opportunity to write down those golden nuggets of relationship wisdom for the lovely bride-to-be.

Enjoy a lot of:

_____

_____

_____

_____

_____

Make time for:

_____

_____

_____

_____

_____

A good wife should always:

_____

_____

_____

_____

Never back down on:

_____

_____

_____

_____

Stop and think before you:

_____

_____

_____

_____

A wife needs time to/for:

_____

_____

A husband needs time to/for:

_____

_____

_____

_____

It's not uncommon to:

_____

_____

_____

_____

Surround yourself with:

_____

_____

_____

_____

If in doubt, go ahead and:

_____

_____

And if you're really stumped on advice, here are a few ready-made tips for a healthy and happy(ish) marriage!

◊ Just say, 'Yes, Dear.' And then do whatever the hell you like.

◊ Keep that flame burnin', baby: once a month, enjoy a hubby-and-wife date night.

◊ Believe. Achieve.

◊ Never go to bed stewing on an argument.

◊ Just take out the bleedin' bins, even if you did it last time.

◊ Love hard and forgive easy.

◊ Compromise is key.

◊ There are no 'winners' or 'losers' in an argument. You guys are in it together.

◊ Never, ever buy gifts at the petrol station.

◊ Don't keep secrets from each other (we're talking the big stuff here, not who ate the last biscuit).

◊ Go for a carrot and stick approach – especially in the bedroom.

◊ Take it in turns to make the dinner.

◊ DON'T DO IT. (Joking, of course.)

Hey, Remember When We ...?

Yes, yes, it's true we've now got Facebook to remind us that we were making a prat of ourselves with our besties in Vodka Revs 'On This Day' back in 2008. But memories are nothing if not personal, and better relayed straight from the horse's mouth.

  Use this page – or grab a separate piece of paper – to write down a special memory or particularly hilarious anecdote between you and the bride. Then why not mix all the hens' memories in a hat, and let the bride guess who each one belongs to!

Friendship isn't a competition, right? But if you *do* want to keep score ... why not have your hens participate in a nice, light-hearted quiz game, putting their knowledge about the bride to the test? For every correct answer, they can bag themselves one glorious hen point. Get sharpening those penis pencils, ladies, it's all to play for!

1. Where did the bride grow up?

_____

2. What is the bride's full name?

_____

3. How many siblings does the bride have?

_____

4. What is the bride's star sign?

_____

5. What was the bride's first job?

_____

_____

6. Who is the bride's favourite celebrity crush?

_____

7. Where did the bride meet her partner?

_____

_____

8. How long has the bride been with her partner?

_____

9. Where did he/she propose?

_____

_____

10. What is the bride's biggest pet peeve?

_____

_____

11. How many wedding dresses did she try on before finding The One?

_____

_____

12. What pet name does the bride use for her partner?

_____

_____

13. What is the bride's favourite film?

_____

_____

14. What is her karaoke song of choice?

_____

_____

15. Where are the happy couple going on honeymoon?

_____

_____

A Photo is Worth a Thousand Words

It could be a while until you get round to that Snappy Snaps trip – *and* there may well be some photos in the hen party album that are for the attendees eyes' only – so pin a pic of your choice here as a keepsake from the Best. Hen. Do. Ever!

◊ Date: . . . .
◊ Location: . . . .
◊ Caption: . . . .

A Very Happy
H-ending

Bring on the Big Day!

So, on a scale of One to Mildly Broken, how are we feeling, hens? You've laughed, you've cried, you've danced, you've bonded, you've 'whooped', you've developed newfound talents for plasticine penis crafting, you've witnessed wildly erotic scenes that are now permanently burnt onto your retinas ... All in all, a bloody good effort! And even if there has been the odd drama between a few flappy hens – hey, you've gotta crack a few eggs to make an omelette!

Pulling off a modern-day hen party is no mean feat. It involves a hell of a lot of gumption, organisation, compromise and stamina. You could say that it's the cultural equivalent of the Duke of Edinburgh Award – just without the satisfaction of any CV-worthy accolades at the end of it (unless, of course, you're the winner of 'Guess the Bum' and thinking of embarking on an investigative career in the Met). But, as the saying goes, the view at the top of the mountain is always worth the climb. And – *by god* – was the look of sheer joy on Auntie Denise's face when she whacked her way to victory in Penis Piñata worth all that extra effort!

And even if a few of the hens are worried they've made a bit of a cock of themselves, never forget: everyone looks back on hen parties with rose-tinted glasses. As with childbirth, there's a specific hen hormone that's injected into the bloodstream once the labour of love has come to an end. It makes any pain and aggro completely void and, in fact, encourages hens to repeat the festivities all over again. What this teaches us, is that the hen do is a seminal part of the circle of life. And it's a flipping good job considering the 16 hen parties you've got lined up in the calendar for next year, right? Talk about survival of the fittest.

But for now you can hang up your L plates with pride and look ahead to the bride's big day, knowing that the excitement stakes have only got higher. You've spent some precious time with the bride's family and BFFs, you've limbered up for a *Strictly*-worthy session on the wedding dance floor (that Beach

Olympics activity is the gift that just keeps on giving), and, most importantly, the bride is feeling well and truly love-bombed. There are plenty of everyday, seemingly small but significant ways that we can show our pals just how much we value them. But hey, life is busy! And – forgive me if I'm overreaching but – nothing injects a little romance into a friendship quite like a hen do. When else is so much love, attention, dedication (and, admittedly, penis) on display? And when else is a bride made to feel like the sexy, lovable hero that she is? I tell you, Beyoncé would be very proud.

So, here's a toast to the modern hen do. You did it, ladies! Now go and get some much-needed kip – we'll see you at the wedding ...

NOTES

NOTES

_____
_____
_____
_____
_____
_____
_____
_____
_____
_____
_____
_____
_____
_____
_____
_____
_____
_____
_____
_____

NOTES

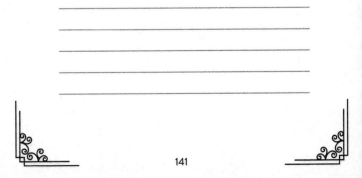

NOTES

NOTES

NOTES

_____
_____
_____
_____
_____
_____
_____
_____
_____
_____
_____
_____
_____
_____
_____
_____
_____
_____
_____
_____
_____
_____